# Fishing for angels

## THE MAGIC OF KITES

# *Fishing for angels*
## THE MAGIC OF KITES

*David Evans*

*Illustrated by Adele D'Arcy*

**ANNICK PRESS LTD.**
Toronto, Canada

Design Brian Bean

Edited by Adele D'Arcy

Annick Press Ltd.

Annick Press gratefully acknowledges the support of The Canada Council and the Ontario Arts Council.

**Canadian Cataloguing in Publication Data**

Evans, David, 1963–
Fishing for angels: the magic of kites

ISBN 1-55037-162-2

1. Kites—Juvenile literature.   2. Kites—Juvenile fiction.   I. D'Arcy, Adele.
II. Title.

TL759.5.E83 1991     j629.133'32     C90-095315-2

Distributed in Canada and the USA by:
Firefly Books Ltd.
250 Sparks Avenue
Willowdale, Ontario M2H 2S4

The text in this book was set in Bodoni and Univers
The illustrations were rendered in ink, gouache and collage

Printed and bound in Canada by
D.W. Friesen & Sons Ltd.
∞ Printed on acid-free paper

*For Phoebe, Just Because*

# Table of Contents

# Acknowledgements

A fair amount of "luck" allowed this project to come to fruition; however, there are some folk who don't believe in happenstance or luck, and I would like to thank them for their encouragement and support: Mike Griffith, for his excitement and belief in the project before I had realized what I'd gotten myself into; Naomi Woodspring, despite the voodoo dolls; Ray and Peggy Wismer—without them I'd have never taken "go fly a kite" to heart; Skye Morrison for her library and Chinese tea; Roland Falk, of tako tako; the Desjardins family for their kind criticism; Anna Camilleri, my "writing partner"; the staff of the children's section at the North York Public Library; *Kite Lines* magazine, especially Simon Freidin; The Museum for Textiles, Toronto; Adele D'Arcy, my editor and illustrator; and my Mum and Dad, Anne and Dave Evans, for their great enthusiasm and support, and the occasional bus ticket home.

◆

# Introduction

There is a North American Native saying that goes, "During all the time that I am feeling sorry for myself, a Great Spirit carries me through the sky." To the ancient Greeks, 'pneuma' meant both 'spirit' and 'wind'.

Kites are a symbol of respect for this 'great spirit'. Someone once told me that he felt as if he were fishing for angels when he flew his kite. Perhaps this isn't as far-fetched as it may seem. While kites are used mainly for sports and recreation in the Western world, in many Eastern cultures they have kept the spiritual significance connected with their origins. Throughout history, kites have also been used to enable people to fly—a magical feat not unlike that which angels have always been able to do.

I'd like to share some of the magic of this ancient pastime with you in this collection of facts and stories about kites.

◆

# FAT ONE AND ROOSTER

Kite-flying is an ancient tradition in China, and many people think that kites originated there. For hundreds of years, the Chinese celebrated Kite Day on the ninth day of the ninth moon with kite-flying festivals. It was thought that flying a kite then would bring good luck. Here is a story of what happened on one of those special days long ago.

Fat One and Rooster were two old wise men who wandered the countryside, relying on the good will of simple folk for their food and lodging. They had only two possessions each: their ragged, old robes that protected them during the day and kept them warm at night, and their paper kites, beautifully decorated with coloured inks. Both men were given to long discourses, and over the years, they had solved between them all the problems of the world and determined the reason for the rising of the sun and the setting of the moon.

◆

Fat One and Rooster had a favourite day of the year, and that was Kite Day. Every year they looked forward to yet another opportunity to fly their kites and ruminate on the dippings and swayings of their winged toys. One year, the two old sages went up into the mountains, away from all other people, to celebrate Kite Day in seclusion. They found a peaceful mountain meadow alive with the buzzing of insects and the gentle swaying of brightly coloured meadow flowers. The wind was calm and steady, and with very little effort, the two old men launched their kites.

When their kites were firmly fixed in the sky, they lay back on the grass and began to debate on the topic of virtue. Presently they decided that the only path to truth and enlightenment lay in ridding oneself of one's earthly possessions, no matter how unpretentious or innocent. They decided to let loose their kites, thus freeing themselves of the last remaining obstacle in their paths toward inner peace.

But Rooster was a tricky fellow. While Fat One was busy setting free his kite, he tied his own kite string to his big toe. Fat One let go of his kite and turned to look at Rooster. When he saw Rooster's sly smile and the kite line tied around Rooster's big toe, he leapt up and scuttled after his own kite, whose string was floating lazily across the meadow. Rooster let out a sharp cry and ran after Fat One, who in his hurry hadn't noticed that he was charging headlong toward the edge of a cliff. With a desperate leap, Rooster grabbed Fat One by his robe, almost tearing it off him in the process. The men tumbled together, coming to a rest at the cliff's edge.

Panting, they watched Fat One's kite drift out over the valley and out of sight. Rooster pulled in his own which was still attached to his big toe. He looked solemnly at Fat One and presented him with his own kite.

"I give you my kite," said Rooster, "as a lesson and a reminder that you shouldn't be so keen to sacrifice your last earthly possession for the sake of your kite."

# ORIGIN OF KITES

No one knows for sure where kites first came from, but it seems that they were first known in the South Sea islands. Even today some natives of the Soloman Islands in the Pacific Ocean use kites as a fishing aid, flying them from the backs of their canoes with a line dangling from them.

Their main catch were bonito and garfish, and for bait they attached to the tail of the kite a web from the silk-spinning spider. The kite itself was made of sago palm, and as it flew, it lightly dragged the bait across the surface of the water, attracting the fish and entangling them. Feeling a tug on the line, the person fishing would then pull in the catch.

Early kites built in the Pacific islands were intended mainly to catch fish, so little time was wasted constructing them. Generally they consisted of a single leaf with twigs serving as a brace. In some places, instead of a thick spider's web, a hook made of wood, bone or sometimes even jade was used.

Though kite fishing is rarely practised today by the indigenous peoples of the Pacific Islands, it is gaining popularity in Europe and the Americas as a sport. Modern fishing tackle has overcome some of the problems experienced by early kite-fishers.

In the Polynesian islands, kites were closely associated with the gods, especially the god Tane, who is often pictured as a kite, and the god Rongo, the patron saint of the arts, kites and kite flying. It was believed that through these gods kites came into being. Tane is sometimes known as "Tane Mahuta", or Tane the Flyer. The story is told that Tane challenged his brother Rongo to a competition to see who could fly his kite the high-

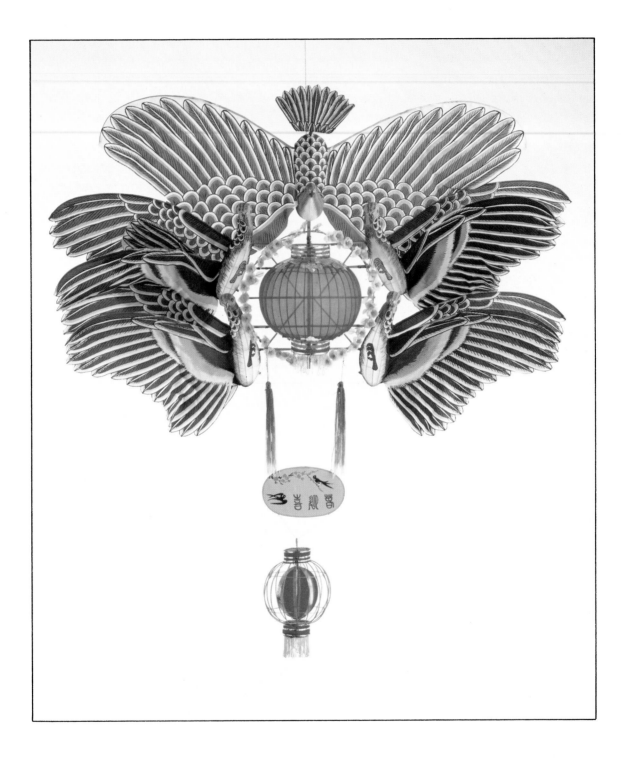

est. Much to Tane's chagrin, Rongo had discovered a vast quantity of string, and it was he who won the contest. From this first use of kites, humans discovered how to fly kites, as well as the delight of kite flying competitions. At the start of each kite flying game, the first kite would bear Rongo's name, and would be flown in his honour.

From the Polynesian islands knowledge of kites spread to Aotearea or what is known in the West as New Zealand. Aotearea is the name given to their homeland by the Maori, the islands' indigenous people.

The Maori most often made their kites in the shape of manu, the Maori word for 'bird'. They believed that birds could carry messages between humans and the gods. Sometimes their kites represented the gods themselves. The Maori god Rehua is depicted as a bird, and was thought to be the ancestor of all kites.

Because kite flying was considered a sacred ritual, it was often accompanied by a type of chant called a turu manu. This chant usually emphasized the connection between the kite and nature. The Maori believed that chanting a turu manu would cause a kite to carry to other lands the prestige of the tribe flying it. The following is a translation of a turu manu:

*My bird, by power of charm ascending,*
*In the glance of an eye, like the sparrow hawk,*
*By this charm shall my bird arise,*
*My bird bestride the heavens.*
*Beyond the swirling waters,*
*Like the stars Atutahi and Rehua,*
*And there spread out thy wings,*
*To the very clouds. Truly so.*

The Maori also used kites to discover the will of the gods, or to predict the future. This practice is known as divination. They believed that by watching the flight of a kite they could know what was going to happen in the future. For example, if a kite were to crash, and a terrible event occurred soon afterwards, it was thought that this was foreshadowed by the kite's poor performance. By the same token, if a kite were to fly high and well preceding a happy occurrence, it was thought that this too had been foretold. Some sources say that if a kite was seen flying near a village, it was a sign of peace. Also, if a kite was somehow associated with the death of a person, the kite was named after that person.

Kite flying as a source of spiritual inspiration and divination has almost completely died out, although there have been recent efforts amongst the Maori to resurrect this ancient art form.

There are very few original Maori kites in existence. Those which do exist are for the most part in museums or private collections. From those that survive, it is possible to tell what materials were used in their construction.

A variety of local plants were used. Aute, or paper mulberry, was used to construct the sail, as was raupo, a type of bullrush. Kareao, a woody vine, was then split to make a durable, supple frame. Kites were decorated with many different things. Charcoal and red ochre were used for colouring. Feathers from birds such as the albatross, the Australian Harrier and the wood pigeon were used. Often shells, in particular paua shells, were used as decorations. Streamers and tails were also attached.

Flying lines were often made of lengths of split flax tied together to make a rope. To this line were attached "kite climbers" or "kite messengers"—wind blown objects, such as leaves—that would travel up the kite line.

Some Maori kites possessed a false "head". The head was often filled with shells to make a rattle, and had horns made from raupo stalks. There have been examples of other kites found with false heads sporting beards made of dog hair, and one has been discovered with a shark's tooth hanging from its ear!

Two of these so-called "Bird Man" kites are known to still exist, one in the Auckland Institute and Museum, the other in London's British Museum. Both are shaped as a flying creature with the body, legs and wings of a bird and the head of a human. The head of one of these kites is covered with raupo leaves, the other has a frame of manuka, or teatree, and is covered with a linen fabric. Both have shell decorations and elaborate ink "tattoos".

China is another place that has been widely accepted as the birthplace of kites. There is a story of a Chinese general named Huan Theng who, in the year 202 **B.C.E.** watched the way his hat flew from his head, and from this got the idea for a particular military strategy. During a battle, he found his army surrounded by the enemy. He built a large number of kites and fit them with thin pieces of bamboo that hummed and shrieked in the wind. Late one night, he and his army flew these kites over the encampment of the opposing army. The kites screamed and shrieked in the wind, frightening the enemy terribly, and causing them to flee, convinced that evil spirits were out to destroy them.

Both the Chinese and the Japanese learned to use kites for raising soldiers into the air as spies or snipers using bows and arrows. Old Chinese and Japanese prints depict these warriors flying over enemy territory.

It seems, however, that warriors were not the only ones who had discovered the usefulness of kites. There is a story from Japan about the famous robber Kakinoki Kinsuke. He was supposed to have used a person-lifting kite to raise himself up to the roof of Nagoya Castle where there were statues of dolphins made of gold. He was able to steal some of the scales from the dolphins, and was even

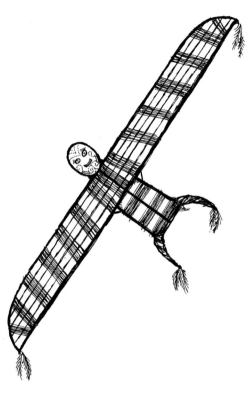

**A Maori "Bird Man" kite.**

able to land safely with the stolen gold, but his story has a rather unpleasant ending. The authorities did not appreciate him stealing from a sacred place, so he was arrested and executed. As we will see later, the Europeans expanded on the idea of the person-lifting kite.

As kites became popular throughout Asia, they were incorporated into the local customs. For example, in Korea it is a tradition to write the names and birthdates of male children on kites and then fly them. The kite line is cut so the kite will fly away. It is thought that so doing will take away bad luck and evil spirits and ensure a good year.

For hundreds of years, kites have played a significant role in the spiritual life of the people of Thailand. Each Thai monarch had her or his own kite which was flown continuously during the winter months by imperial monks and priests working in shifts. Kites in flight were also used to decorate the royal palace in Bangkok.

Kites are also flown by the people of Thailand during the time of the **monsoons**. The kites are supposed to send their prayers to the gods, asking them to blow away

**A traditional**

**Japanese kite.**

the monsoon rainclouds and save their crops from flooding.

In Japan there is another tradition that involves **windsocks**, cousins of the kite. These windsocks are in the shape of fish, the carp to be specific. The carp is a fish that returns to breed at the place it was born, overcoming great obstacles in order to do so. To the Japanese they are a symbol of fortitude and great strength of will. The windsocks, called **Koi Nabori**, are flown on May 5th, which is Children's Day. The qualities represented by the carp are meant as an inspiration to children.

# THE SHEPHERD BOY

Some legends were created in order to explain the origins of various things. This story from Bali explains the origins of kites. The Balinese believe that the first kite was a feather plucked from the neck of a long-necked goose. With the help of both this feather and the wind, a young shepherd boy was able to discover his destiny. Today, one of the sacred aspects of kite flying in Bali is to remember this shepherd boy, and the Hindu gods **Vishnu** and **Siva**.

The shepherd leaned back against the tree and breathed in the fragrance of the sweet field grasses. Through half-open eyes he watched his bull methodically grazing in the field. The warmth of the sun relaxed him, and gave him a sense of well-being. Soon he began to doze, allowing his mind to wander. In his mind's eye he saw a beautiful young woman, her long black hair caught up in a thick glossy braid. Her skin was

♦

smooth and brown and her flashing friendly eyes were as black as night-velvet.

The shepherd roused himself and reached for a leather pouch he'd brought along with him. Within, he found a small pot of ink, a long quill and a fresh sheet of parchment, and he began to sketch the young woman he'd created in his imagination. In little time the image of the woman in his daydream appeared on the paper. The shepherd smiled, pleased with himself.

Suddenly a shadow fell upon the parchment. With a start the shepherd looked up to behold the king of the land staring down at him.

"Who is that beautiful young girl?" demanded the king, pointing down at the shepherd's drawing. His voice was sharp and impatient.

"She lives in my heart, sire," stammered the shepherd, at once terrified and awed by the sight of the king enwrapped in his magnificent silks. "She lives but in my imagination."

The king smiled wickedly. "I demand that you bring her to me, for I mean to make her my queen!"

"But Your Majesty!" cried the shepherd, "she is not a woman of flesh and bone, but a vapour, a fantasy of my own creation!"

"And yet I intend to make her my queen and my wife," the king snarled, moving his face menacingly close to the shepherd's. "If you should fail to bring her to me by tomorrow's sunset, you shall pay with your life!" The king laughed, leaving the shepherd quaking.

The poor shepherd didn't know what to do. How could he find the young woman when she was nothing more than a winged shadow, a flight of his fancy? It was impossible, he knew. With his mind whirling in confusion and fear, he leapt up and stumbled into the forest. His only chance of surviving the king's wrath was to escape from the island.

For hours the shepherd blundered through the forest, the tears coursing down his cheeks, until in exhaustion he collapsed under a mahogany tree. He closed his eyes and slowly concentrated on regaining his breath and clearing his mind. As he calmed himself, he became aware of a presence behind him. Terrified that it might be the king or one of his manservants, he pitched himself forward and twisted around to look. There stood a monster, a huge blue hairy beast with enormously

♦

broad shoulders, a red mane like a lion's and long daggersharp teeth. The shepherd was horrified, but when he saw the gentleness of the monster's large green eyes, the fear quickly subsided and was replaced with respect.

"I know why you are running, Shepherd," said the monster in a low rumble, reaching out and touching the shepherd's head. "I can help you if you wish. You will not need to leave this island, your home, if you choose to follow my advice."

The shepherd was calmed by the deep timbre of the monster's voice, and the warmth of its hand on his head was like the healing rays of the sun. He felt he could trust the monster completely.

"I do believe that you can help me," he told the monster, "and I trust you not to lead me astray."

"Very well, then," replied the monster, "my suggestion is simple." The monster reached under a flowering bush and there he found a long-necked goose. With the same care that he had shown the shepherd, he gently caressed the bird. Then he deftly plucked a pure white feather from the goose's neck.

"Follow this feather wherever the wind takes it," he told the shepherd. "The wind shall not fail you if you continue to believe and trust." With that, the monster held the feather up and blew on it, sending it floating up into the trees. The shepherd hardly dared to take the time to thank the monster. He quickly ran after the feather and followed it as it darted between the trees. He could feel a breeze gently blowing against his back, yet at times it seemed that the feather ignored the wind, hovering for a few moments to allow the shepherd to catch up to it. And then it would be off again.

The shepherd followed the feather out of the forest and over rice paddies and meadows toward a mountain that was covered with a lushness of trees and bushes festooned with brightly coloured blossoms. The shepherd reached the mountain as the sun was setting, and for a moment he was afraid he would lose sight of the feather in the darkness of night. But the feather seemed to carry its own light, and with the help of the moonlight, the shepherd easily followed it up the mountain. He marvelled at how he didn't seem to tire if he concentrated solely on the feather floating in front of him.

All night long he followed the feather, until, just as dawn threw her majestically coloured cape over the sky, he reached the top of the mountain. There the feather stopped, glowing brightly, and the shepherd sat down on the ground, wondering and waiting.

As the feather continued to glow, it seemed to the shepherd that he could hear singing, a beautiful music that came from beyond the lavender-hued clouds. The feather glowed more intensely as the singing grew louder, and the shepherd caught his breath. The breezes tugged around him, catching up his hair and swirling it around, as the wind from scores of wings tossed the feather gently on its current. Spirits, or **devas**, appeared from behind the morning clouds, and hovered singing, over the mountain top.

The shepherd was speechless. He had never seen such beautiful beings. All of them, male and female, were wonderfully attired in exotically coloured batiks and feathers. A myriad of colour, turquoise, scarlet, orange and violet, seemed to move the sky in a living rainbow. From their ears and around their necks, the devas wore gems of all sorts and garlands of brilliantly coloured flowers. The deva closest to the shepherd touched his hand. The shepherd gasped, for she was the image of the young woman he had first seen in his mind and had then sketched on parchment. In his heart he thanked the monster. Then he explained his situation to her.

"If I do not deliver you to the king by sundown, he shall kill me, for he means to make you his wife. Can you help?"

"Do you believe that the feather the monster gave you has led you in the right direction?" the deva asked the shepherd, her face kindly and her eyes sparkling.

"Yes, indeed I do," the shepherd answered her.

"Then continue to trust," she said, and placed a calming hand on his heart.

Suddenly there was an uncanny stillness in the air. The devas stopped singing and turned their faces in unison toward the sky.

"Siva comes," whispered the deva to the shepherd and squeezed his hand encouragingly.

And Siva did come. A radiant cloud began to quickly swirl in upon itself, spinning faster and faster, until the shape of the god began to take form. With a flash of light, and a sound like a thousand deeply toned drums resounding and drowning out all else, the great god Siva appeared. He was truly an awe-inspiring figure, and the shepherd remembered, ashamed, how he had let the king strike fear into his heart. For beside Siva, the king, a human being no different than the shepherd himself, seemed no longer frightening. As his awe and amazement at the swiftly approaching god grew, so did the shepherd's courage. The immense form of the god blocked out the light of the morning sun, yet Siva, like the feather and the devas, glowed with an inner intensity that lit up all that was around him. The feather continued to hover amongst them, as Siva looked down at the shepherd.

"Shepherd, I have watched you for a long time, and I have presented you with this test of your trust. Truly you are worthy to be a descendent of Vishnu, and indeed that is what you are. And by his name you are the rightful king of this land."

◆

The shepherd stared in breathless excitement at the god, and then at the beautiful deva beside him.

"And the sweet deva who is now at your side," continued Siva, "if it be her will, is to become your queen and partner, and together you shall rule over this land."

At this, the deva glanced at the shepherd and gently squeezed his hand. Then with great reverence, she looked at the god Siva and said "Yes, it is my will."

"Then the great Vishnu decrees it, and I sanctify it," answered Siva. "And as for the usurper who now calls himself king," the god continued, "he is already destroyed. I have sent the monster, he who plucked for you the goose-feather, and he has killed the false king. The land is from this moment on rightfully yours to rule."

So it was that the shepherd and the deva were married, and became king and queen. To celebrate their liberation from the evil king and honour the new king and queen, the people of the land flew kites that looked like the magic goose-feather. And this they do to this very day.

# SOLDIERS AND INVENTORS

eople are no more certain as to when and how kites were first introduced into Europe than they are of the origins of kites. There are several theories, however.

For example, it has been recorded that around 400 B.C.E. a Greek named Archylas of Tarentum built and flew a wooden bird-shaped object that may have been a kite. It is known that such kites were flown in China, so perhaps he had had some contact with that country.

Another theory is that Dutch and Portuguese traders dealing with merchants in Japan and China brought back kites. It is common to see Japanese fighter kites, the **Nagasaki Hata**, sporting the colours of the Dutch flag.

There are records of windsock-like banners used by the Romans called dracos. They were used during military and religious celebrations, and appeared in the later years of the Empire. It is quite possible that the Romans got the idea from the Persians who used them many centuries before. The draco was a long windsock-like banner attached to a pole. It had a carved, three-dimensional dragon's head decorated with lamps. In a strong breeze the body would billow out, giving the whole banner the appearance of a dragon in flight. Tapestries from the Middle Ages depict draco-like banners being flown. It is also interesting to note that in several European languages the word for 'kite' is very similar to the word 'draco'.

Kites were also used at one time by Europeans to flush game from thickets while hunting, but this proved to be awkward and was quickly abandoned.

However kites were first introduced into Europe, it really wasn't until the 16th and 17th centuries that they became a common item in everyday life. Some paintings of the time show dragon kites being flown, but generally the more common pear-shape or diamond-shape is depicted. The military and religious significance of kites had disappeared, and kite flying was considered a frivolous pastime.

Things began to change in the 18th century when adults began to recognize the scientific value kites possessed. Children, however, had never doubted their value in the first place.

Benjamin Franklin began flying kites for the sheer fun of it. Once he allowed himself to be towed almost two kilometres across a lake while floating on his back. Little did he know that 150 years later, Samuel Cody would tow a boat across the English Channel using kites.

In June 1752, in Philadelphia, Franklin used a kite to determine the electrical nature of clouds. Taking advantage of a summer storm, he went out into a field to a hut he had constructed specifically for the experiment. The kite flew for quite some time before it showed any signs of having been

**A modern person-lifting kite.**

electrified. He was about to give up when he noticed a few loose threads of the hemp rope he was using as a flying line were standing erect and trying to avoid one another as though they had some sort of electric charge. In excitement he touched a key he had tied to the flying line and immediately saw a small electric spark. After the flying line had become wet and acted as a better conductor, the sparks flew! Franklin's experiments were extremely important in the quest to harness electricity.

Kites were also used by meteorologists to lift measuring instruments. Two years before Franklin's famous experiment, Dr. Alexander Wilson of Edinburgh used a kite to take aloft a thermometer to determine air temperature at high altitudes. In the 1880's, an English scientist named E.D. Archibald used anemometers lifted by kites to measure wind speeds at various altitudes.

Another famous inventor and kite enthusiast was Dr. Alexander Graham Bell, who is best known for having invented the telephone. Like Franklin, he used kites to study the weather. He was also interested in discovering a way to enable people to fly, and experimented with kites to learn more about the possibilities of flight.

Bell was born in Edinburgh in 1847, but moved to Canada in 1870. He became moderately wealthy through his invention of the telephone.

Bell built a home in Baddeck, Nova Scotia named Beinn Bhreagh, which is Gaelic for Beautiful Mountain. It was here in the late 1800's that he first started his experiments in flight.

Soon he had developed a kite that could raise a person off the ground solely under the power of the wind. He also worked on developing a kite that could take both a person and an engine into the air. He developed the **tetrahedral cell**, which had an amazing strength for such a light structure.

It wasn't until 1907 that Bell used tetrahedral cells to raise a man into the air. He built a huge kite called the Cygnet, which had 3,393 cells. Lt. Thomas E. Selfridge was the passenger. Both he and the kite were towed behind a steamer in the waters of Baddeck Bay. Though the flight only lasted minutes, the Cygnet proved to be extraordinarily strong.

Excited with his success with the

◆

**A multi-cell box kite, similar to Cody's inventions.**

Cygnet, Bell built Cygnet II, which was meant to carry both a person and an engine. Unfortunately it wasn't possible to develop a suitably light engine. Although the Cygnet II was the last of Dr. Bell's experiments with kites, he had contributed immensely to the knowledge of flight. A museum at Baddeck, Nova Scotia, houses quite a few of his kites.

Bell was one of the founding members of the Aerial Experiment Association, an organization dedicated to enabling people to fly. Though the first airplane was invented by the Wright brothers, the A.E.A. developed four planes of its own.

The Wright brothers, Orville and Wilbur, used kites in their experiments and based their early airplane prototypes on their knowledge of kites. The German inventor, Otto Lilienthal, also used kites in the development of his person-lifting gliders, as did the French aviator, Octave Chanute.

Probably the most colourful of kite enthusiasts was the inventor and showman Samuel Franklin Cody of Birdville, Texas. He spent the early years of his life as cowboy and wild horse trainer, and later became a gold prospector around the Yukon and Klondike Rivers. He eventually earned his living touring the United States as "Captain Cody, King of the Cowboys". He adopted his image from his friend and mentor William Frederick Cody, known as "Buffalo Bill". In 1890 he moved to England and became famous for his Wild West shows.

Cody's son Leon was a kite enthusiast, and sometime near the end of the 19th century Cody himself took an interest in kites. Leon and "Captain" Cody competed with each other, building increasingly larger kites that were able to climb to ever increasing heights.

The elder Cody developed a type of winged box kite from which he devised a system that was able to lift a person into the air. He approached the British military authorities, suggesting that kites could be used to send aloft a soldier equipped with a camera and a firearm. The army initially refused his suggestions.

However, after a successful crossing of the English Channel in a small boat pulled by his "Cody Kites", the British army finally expressed interest, and adopted the system for observation. Eventually the Russian navy and the French army adopted observation systems based on Cody's kites.

At the same time that Cody was flying his person-lifters, B.F.S. Baden-Powell, brother of the founder of the Boy Scouts, was developing his own lifters. He developed an apparatus consisting of a basket attached to a train of kites.

The British army decided to use Baden-Powell's invention in 1895 during the Boer War. However, by the time the system was prepared and transported to southern Africa, the war had ended, so it was never actually used.

Kites were used during First World War for trench observation and lifting signal flags. In World War II, the U.S. army also used kites designed to resemble airplanes for target practice.

Today, many of the innovative kites developed with military and scientific purposes in mind are used in kite festivals and competitions.

# MAUI'S KITE

Long ago in Hawaii people told stories to explain the wonders of nature. This story is about Maui, who wanted to tame the winds.

The weather had been first warm and then cool that month. There was a feeling of uncertainty, of change, of excitement in the air that inspired Maui, and he decided to build a kite.

And what a kite it was! For a sail, his mother gave him her largest, strongest piece of **barkcloth**. For cross-pieces he used great lengths of bamboo carefully cut and notched. And from the **olona** shrub he cut long lengths of branch, twisting them together to make a strong rope. With great care he constructed his kite.

Maui's kite was a work of art. His friends excitedly gathered around to help him carry it to Keeper-of-the-Winds. Maui and the others paraded through the village, and all the people left their work and came to watch.

◆

To the Cave-of-the-Winds they marched. As they approached the cave they could see Keeper-of-the-Winds sitting by the entrance.

"O Keeper-of-the-Winds," cried Maui, "come, bring Ipu Iki, the small gourd that holds the gentle breezes, and let us fly our kite!"

Keeper-of-the-Winds was a wise old woman, and knew that the gentle winds of Ipu Iki would play kindly with the boy. She went into her cave and returned, carrying a small calabash, or hollowed-out gourd.

"The name of this calabash is Ipu Iki," she said, "and it holds the gentle winds; the soft, the misty and the dusty." And she sang her song,

*O Wind, Soft Wind of **Hilo**,*
*Wind from the calabash of everlasting winds,*
*come from Ipu Iki.*
*O Wind, Soft Wind of Hilo,*
*Come gently, come with mildness.*

The lid of the calabash began to stir, and Keeper-of-the-Winds carefully lifted its edge. Slowly Soft Wind of Hilo drifted out and tugged at the kite. Maui let out some cord and his friends held up the great sail, but the wind could do no more than rustle the cloth. Again Keeper-of-the-Winds sang her song,

*O Wind, Misty Wind of **Waimea**,*
*Wind from the calabash of everlasting winds,*
*come from Ipu Iki.*
*O Wind, Misty Wind of Waimea,*
*hasten to me, come to me with strength.*

Again the lid of the calabash stirred, and Keeper-of-the-Winds raised it slightly. Misty Wind of Waimea flew out, sweeping the kite from the hands of Maui's friends, sending it soaring over the trees.

Maui's friends cheered as he let out the cord, and even Keeper-of-the-Winds became excited. She called Dusty Wind and Smoky Wind. The kite soared like a great bird out over the sea. Maui leaned back and laughed in happiness as Keeper-of-the-Winds stood silently and looked with pleasure upon the boy's face, and then at the kite.

"That's enough for today," said Keeper-of-the-Winds. "One must respect the winds; they should not be taken for granted. They will respect you if you respect them."

After a few moments silence, Maui slowly nodded his head. "Yes, O Keeper-of-the-Winds," he said a little reluctantly. "Call your winds back to you."

Keeper-of-the-Winds removed the lid from Ipu Iki and called back her winds. Slowly the kite dropped, and as Maui reeled in the line, his friends caught the kite. Keeper-of-the-Winds put the lid back on the calabash, and everyone went home.

But Maui was not content. He had seen how high his kite had gone, but wondered just how much higher it could fly. He remembered the words of Keeper-of-the-Winds, and knew that he must respect the winds, but still he wondered.

The next day Maui and his friends took the great kite and went back to Cave-of-the-Winds. They found Keeper-of-the-Winds sitting out front.

"O Keeper-of-the-Winds, bring out Ipu Nui, calabash of the Four Great Winds!" cried out Maui.

"The winds of Ipu Iki were enough, Maui," said the old woman. "Do you not remember what I said to you? You must respect the winds, especially the Four Great Winds."

"But I am strong, as strong as the Four Winds," said Maui, only half believing his own words, and he began to chant,

*O Winds, mighty as the gods,*
*Wind from the calabash of everlasting winds,*
*come from Ipu Nui.*
*Strong Wind of the East,*
*churning Wind of the North,*
*hasten and come to me.*

From inside the cave came a mighty roar. Keeper-of-the-Winds started and ran towards the entrance, but she was greeted by North Wind and East Wind, who bowled her over and snatched the kite from the hands of Maui's friends. Maui leaned back as far as he could as the kite was swept far out over the sea. He laughed with delight when he saw how far his kite had gone, and at Keeper-of-the-Winds who was struggling vainly to put

35

the lid back on Ipu Nui. But with a great screaming and howling West Wind and South Wind roared out of the calabash, knocking it from the woman's hands and sending it rolling away.

The kite went as high as the cord was long, and still it tugged violently. The cord began to hum in the wind, and as the sky grew dark, the kite disappeared into the clouds.

Thinking himself to be in control, Maui called out, "O Winds, mighty as the gods, return to Ipu Nui."

But of course the winds were beyond his control. The sky darkened. The four howling winds raged stronger and stronger until the cord attached to the kite snapped with a mighty crack, sending Maui reeling backwards. The kite sailed away over the mountain, never to be seen again.

Yet the winds continued to rage. The palms that grew around Cave-of-the-Winds bent down their heads in the face of the onslaught, until they too broke. Over the entire island the winds screamed and howled. The

sheets of barkcloth set out to dry were blown away and a heavy rain began, flooding the fields, sending the men scurrying in all directions. The winds had proven who was the stronger.

In desperation Keeper-of-the-Winds pounced on Ipu Nui and took it back to the cave, walking bent double into the driving wind and rain. She sat in the cave and worked the night, gently coaxing the winds back into the calabash. Finally the storm ended.

Maui was in disgrace, and people started to call him He-Who-Brought-the-Great-Storm. The people would have nothing to do with him. His friends left him and Keeper-of-the-Winds looked the other way when Maui came to visit.

Finding himself alone with nothing to do, Maui built another kite, smaller than the first, and flew it near his home when there was no-one else about. He would tie the kite to a rock and study its movements in the sky, and soon he could tell when the weather would be fine, or stormy. One day he noticed some men going off to the fields.

"It will rain today," said Maui to the men. "Tomorrow will be a better day to work the fields."

But the men just scowled at him. Soon it did begin to rain, and the men came running back to the village, looking in amazement at Maui as they ran by.

Another day Maui warned a group of women that their barkcloth could be blown from its drying place, because his kite told him that there would be a storm that day. The women paid him no attention. Soon, however, they were out of their yards, chasing the cloth which was blowing about in the storm.

In time, the village people began to rely on Maui and his kite. He taught them how to predict for themselves from the dancing movements of the kite which days would be good for planting, or fishing, or drying barkcloth. People stopped calling Maui He-Who-Brought-the-Great-Storm and started calling him Teacher-and-Foreteller-of-the-Weather. Keeper-of-the-Winds became friendly towards him again, but Maui had learned his lesson. Never again did he call for the winds of Ipu Iki or Ipu Nui.

# KITES TODAY

Today kite festivals are held in almost every country of the world. Some, like those in India and the Far East, have ancient roots.

The Indian city of Ahmedabad has a history of kite festivals. Situated about 200 miles north of Bombay, Ahmedabad is famous for its annual **Makar Sankranti** festival, also known as **Uttarayan** or **Uttran**. Every January 14th, people from all over the city fly kites from rooftops to celebrate the end of the winter.

Makar Sankranti means "the conclusion of Capricorn", the astrological sign that prevails over the winter solstice. The Indians celebrate the time when the sun passes from Capricorn to Aquarius, as it is certain now that winter is ending and the gods are awakening after their long sleep. While the festival in Ahmedabad is famous all over the world, smaller festivals take place throughout India.

For weeks before the festival almost every store or market stall sells fighter kites. Even the poorest people take part in the celebration, making their kites from whatever materials they can find.

The fighter kites are made of thin tissue paper and decorated with feathers and whistles that emit a piercing shriek. They are flown on manja, a cotton line coated with a mixture of ground glass and glue. The object of using this type of string is to cut the strings of as many of the other kites as possible. The skies over the city are ablaze with the colour of thousands of kites, each vying for space and each out to cut the flying lines of the others. However, this aerial battle is undertaken with a good humour and no feelings of ill-will.

The Japanese also developed a kite called the Nagasaki Hata. It is a type of fighter kite that is very quick and highly manoeuverable. The kite's design is based on that of the Indian fighter kite, such as those flown in the Ahmedabad festival.

Kite flying in Thailand is serious business. It is a professional sport, complete with championships, leagues and teams, and 72 rules enforced by umpires. An annual competition is held on the Royal Cremation Ground, and the champion becomes a national hero. Two teams compete; those flying the pakpao, or female kites, and those flying the chula, or male kites. The pakpao kites are small, light and highly manoeuverable, and outnumber the chula kites. They are equipped with nooses with which they try to ensnare the chula. The chula are larger, clumsier kites, but are equipped with sharp talons with which they can entangle the pakpao lines. The playing field is divided by a bamboo fence. Those flying the chula fly from an upwind position across the barrier. To score, a rival's kite must be brought down on the opponent's side of the field. As the smaller pakpao are at a disadvan-

**A foil kite being flown at the festival in Scheveningen.**

tage, twice the amount of points are awarded to a pakpao flyer than to the chula flying opponent if a score is made.

During the Cultural Revolution in China in the late 1960's, kite makers were persecuted and their kites were destroyed. It was believed that they represented a decadent way of life of which the Chinese authorities wanted to rid their society. However, methods of kite making were secretly continued during the harsh times of the Cultural Revolution and kites are coming back into popularity in China. Today there are kite festivals held every year in Beijing and Weifang.

The stunt kite is specifically designed to perform aerobatics. It is a modern descendent of both Indian fighter kites and the inventions of European experimenters such as Bell and Cody. The kite is controlled with two lines, thus two hands are needed to fly it. Stunt kites were originally developed in the familiar diamond shape, but over the last ten years or so, the triangular **delta** shape has been adapted, and a **foil** shaped like an airplane wing has also been developed. These kites are most visually effective if flown in tandem or

**A train of stunt kites.**

in a **train** of several kites connected to one another in a long line. Stunt kites are sometimes used in kite-fishing to troll a line back and forth across a body of water.

Most kite festivals in the West feature stunt flyers in competitions with such diverse categories as 'Smallest Stunter' to 'Longest Train'. Festivals such as the one held in Scheveningen in the Netherlands, or the week-long celebra-

tions in Stuttgart, Germany, are of more recent development than their Eastern counterparts.

However, many common themes run through all these festivals, which attract participants from around the world. The main point is generally not so much to compete and win but to bring alive the romance of kite flying, and to bring together people from various cultures.

# TONY AND NAOMI

Tony MacIntyre had a secret crush on Naomi Quilty. Well, to Naomi it was no secret, but she wasn't saying anything. It was one thing for a boy to have a crush on you, but a whole other thing to admit it, so most of the time she pretended that she just couldn't stand the sight of Tony.

But Tony had this kite, and to him it was one of the best things ever. It was big and shaped like a bat, like the kites you can get at a corner store. The best thing about it was that it was red. Bright red, with big black and yellow eyes.

When he flew it in the farmer's field up by the school, he would dream that he was up there in the sky with Naomi. They'd hold on tight as the kite took them higher and higher. It couldn't happen, he knew, but he figured he could probably ask Naomi to fly the kite with him sometime when nobody was looking.

◆

One Saturday, after he'd helped his dad clean out the garage, and after his dad had dragged him around the hardware store for the ten millionth time, Tony took his kite out for what was left of the afternoon.

He decided he'd just by accident walk by Naomi's house with his kite. Maybe he'd see Naomi playing jumpsies or something.

There was Naomi standing in the driveway, making a pattern in the gravel with the toe of her shoe. Tony's mouth went all dry and his heart felt like it was going to blow up.

He was just about to say, 'Do you want to come help me fly my kite?', when Naomi suddenly said, "Hey Tony! That's a really great kite! Can I go fly it with you?"

Tony could hardly believe his ears, and all he could say was, "Yeah, uh, sure. Come on."

So Naomi ran down the driveway, and the two of them started to walk toward the farmer's field.

"Dad was going to get me to help him pave the driveway this afternoon," Naomi said, "but he fell asleep on the couch. Mom got mad and called him a couch potato, so he's taking her out for dinner. That means I get to do whatever I want."

Tony finally found his tongue, which up until then had been glued to the roof of his mouth. He said, "Oh, well that's good." Taking a deep breath, he said, "I'm glad your dad's a couch potato. I mean, I'm glad we can go fly the kite . . ." then he gulped, ". . . together." She was the prettiest girl he'd ever seen.

Finally they came to the wire fence at the end of the school yard. There was a rumour that if you climbed the fence and went into the field the farmer would get you. Tony had been taking his kite into the field for a long time, and no farmer ever got him, so they didn't worry about it.

The field was muddy and the mud squelched and oozed around their shoes. Once Naomi had to hold Tony up while he put one of his shoes back on as it had been sucked off his foot by some particularly deep mud. Soon they came to a dry place. There was some grass and a few pieces of corn husk lying on the ground. Tony unrolled a length of kite string.

"Okay, you take this that way," he said. There was a strong breeze blowing, so there wasn't going to be any problem getting the kite up.

"Okay," said Naomi. She walked a little way downwind and stopped, holding the kite above her head. With his back to the wind, Tony pulled on the kite string and ran a little way backwards.

"NOW!" he yelled, and Naomi let go of the kite. Immediately it soared into the sky, its wings rattling and vibrating in the wind. It made a whooshing noise as Tony pulled harder on the string, making it fly even higher.

Naomi was jumping up and down yelling "GO! GO!" Tony shouted at her to come and take the string. She ran back to Tony, splashing and sliding in the mud, covering her shoes and socks. She was excited and out of breath when Tony handed the line to her. He showed her how to make the kite dive and climb again by letting out a lot of string and pulling it in hard. She got pretty good at making the kite dance.

"Man, this is so cool!" laughed Naomi. The wind was blowing even harder now, and their hair was flying all over the place. Tony had to shout at her so she could hear him.

"Do you really like it?" he asked her.

When she yelled back, "Oh yeah, it's the greatest!", he said,

"You can have it; it's yours."

Naomi didn't know what to say, but was she ever happy! "Really?" she asked. "You mean it?"

"Yes," Tony said, "Sure."

"Oh thanks! thanks!" said Naomi. "Dad and Mom will probably be ready to go out for dinner and I guess they'll be looking for me," she said as they walked back through the subdivision.

"Yeah, I gotta go home, too, I guess," said Tony. Then he added, "I'm glad you like the kite."

"Oh Tony, it's the best thing anyone has given me in my whole life," Naomi exclaimed. "Thank you!"

When they got to her house, she ran up the driveway, the kite flapping in her hand. She stopped and looked back at Tony, smiled and waved.

"See you on Monday!" she called, and Tony waved back.

When he got home, his mum asked him where his kite was.

"I, uh, I sorta gave it to Naomi," he said.

◆

His mum looked a little surprised. Then she smiled and said, "That was a real nice thing to do, Tony. That kite meant a lot to you."

"Yeah, well, you know, Mum, I kinda like Naomi," he said.

The next day Tony helped his mum cut the lawn. Then his dad got him to wash Squat the dog, so it wasn't until later in the afternoon that he had any time to himself. Soon he found himself on the way to Naomi's house.

As he got closer, he saw that the driveway had been freshly paved. Someone had stuck a red flag on a stick at the end of the driveway to keep people from driving up. But when he actually got to the house, he realized it wasn't a flag at all. It was his kite! Someone had torn up his kite, the best thing he had ever had, and his present to Naomi, and stuck it on a stick at the end of the driveway!

Tony couldn't believe it. "How could someone do that?" he thought. Tears began to well up and burn in his eyes. He turned and ran up the road.

He heard someone yell, "Tony, Tony!" He turned his head and saw Naomi running out of the house, waving her arms. But he just kept running, back to his house, up the stairs and into his bedroom. He slammed the door and threw himself face first onto his bed.

Soon his dad knocked on the door, and asked if he could come in. Tony said he could, and after a few moments he had explained to his dad what had happened. His dad listened to his story, and gave him a hug.

"Tony," he said, "I bet whoever did that didn't realize what they were doing. I bet they didn't know just how important that kite was."

At that moment, his mum called up the stairs, "Tony, there's someone here to see you!"

Tony wiped his eyes and went downstairs with his dad. There in the kitchen were Naomi, and Mr. Quilty, her dad! Naomi's face was red and puffy as if she'd been crying. Mr. Quilty looked a little funny and nervous.

"Hi, Tony," said Mr. Quilty, his voice trembling a bit. "Naomi's just told me about your present to her, and, well, I guess I owe the two of you an apology. I didn't know the kite was a gift from you. I was in such a hurry to get the driveway finished that I just tore it up and stuck it on the stick."

Tony looked at Mr. Quilty and felt a little sorry for him because he looked so nervous. He really looked sorry.

"I was going to buy a new one for Naomi, but it was too late. I'm really sorry, Tony," he said, sticking out his hand to Tony.

Tony took Mr. Quilty's hand and shook it. "That's okay, Mr. Quilty. I guess you didn't know," he said, feeling a little better. Then he saw Naomi smiling at him and felt a lot better.

Suddenly Mr. Quilty seemed to cheer up. "Hey, why don't I drive us down to the hardware store and buy some stuff to build a new kite!" he exclaimed.

"Yeah," said Tony's dad, "when I was a kid we used to build our own.

◆

**47**

I'll come with you."

Tony and Naomi looked at each other and rolled their eyes. "The hardware store, eh Dad?" said Naomi, teasing him.

The dads looked at each other a little blankly, and then started to laugh.

"Come on!" yelled Tony to Naomi, "I'll race you to the car!"

And they ran out the door.

# MAKE YOUR OWN KITE

Kites needn't be complicated or difficult to make. You can make a great looking kite that flies really well for very little money, and if you use your imagination, you'll find all kinds of ways to decorate it. The trick is to keep the kite as light as possible without sacrificing strength. You can use light cotton to make the **sail**, which makes it durable, but if you want to make it out of a paper bag from the grocery store, or a green garbage bag, these will work just as well. It can be an adventure to try and work with materials you might not have considered using, and it'll keep the cost of making your kite down.

On the next few pages you'll find some easy designs for building your own kite.

Use your imagination, and don't be afraid to make mistakes. Part of the fun of making something is learning how to do it, so making a mistake means you have the opportunity to ask questions and learn something new. Have fun!

# EASY-TO-MAKE DIAMOND KITE

This is the kite that probably everyone is familiar with, the "good ol' Charlie Brown" kite. Its shape makes it easy to fly in almost any wind condition, and it can be made in a matter of a few minutes. Try making it with old newspapers or green garbage bags you might have around the house. Brown paper, light cloth or wrapping paper are also good. For the **struts** any light garden stakes, bamboo rods or thin wooden dowelling, about 1 cm or 1/4" in diameter can be used. This kite will need a tail for stability.

## Materials

- ◆ butcher cord or thin garden twine
- ◆ scotch tape or glue
- ◆ 1 sheet of strong paper or light cloth, 102 cm × 102 cm (about 40" × 40")
- ◆ 2 strong, straight sticks of bamboo or wooden dowelling 90 cm (36") and 102 cm (about 40")
- ◆ poster paints, or crayons or felt-tip markers for decorating if you are making the kite from paper.

**1** Make a cross with the two sticks, with the shorter stick placed horizontally across the longer stick. Both sides of the cross-piece should be equal in width.

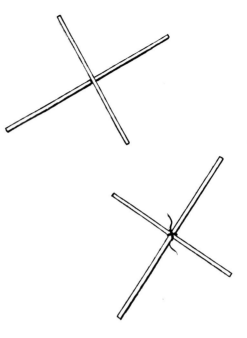

**2** Tie the two sticks together with the string in such a way as to make sure that they are at right angles to each other. A good way to ensure that the joint is strong is to coat it lightly with model cement.

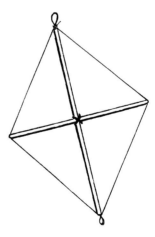

**3** Cut a notch at each end of both sticks. Make it deep enough for the type of string you're using to fit into. Cut a piece of string long enough to stretch all around the kite frame. Make a loop in the top notch and fasten it by wrapping the string around the stick. Stretch the string through the notch at one end of the cross-piece, and make another loop at the bottom. Stretch the string through the notch at the other end of the cross-piece. Finish by wrapping the string a few times around the top of the stick and cutting off what you don't need. To make sure that the string stays in place, put some glue at the end of each stick. This string frame must be taut, but not so tight as to warp the sticks.

**4** Lay the sail material flat on the work surface and place the stick frame face down on top. Cut around it, leaving about 2–3 cm (³/₄"-1") for a margin. Fold these edges over the string frame and tape or glue it down so that the material is tight.

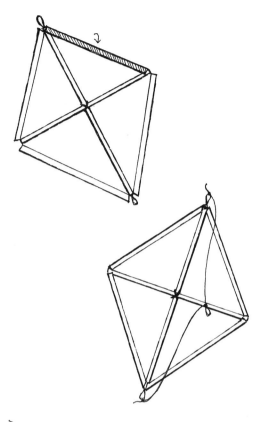

**5** Cut a piece of string about 122 cm (48") long, and tie one end to the loop at the top of the kite. Tie the other end of the string to the loop at the bottom. Tie another small loop in the string just above the intersection of the two cross-pieces. This will be the kite's bridle, the string to which the flying line is attached.

**6** Make a tail by tying a small ribbon made of the same material as the sail roughly every 10 centimetres (4") along a length of string. The tail can be long for high wind conditions, or shorter for light winds. Attach the tail to the loop at the bottom of the kite.

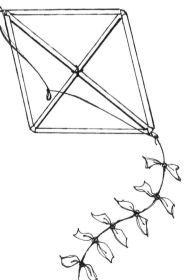

**7** Make a design on the sail of the kite with poster paints, or whatever you want to use to decorate it. You could also use cut-out pieces of construction paper or tissue paper to make a design on the sail, or even pictures from old magazines.

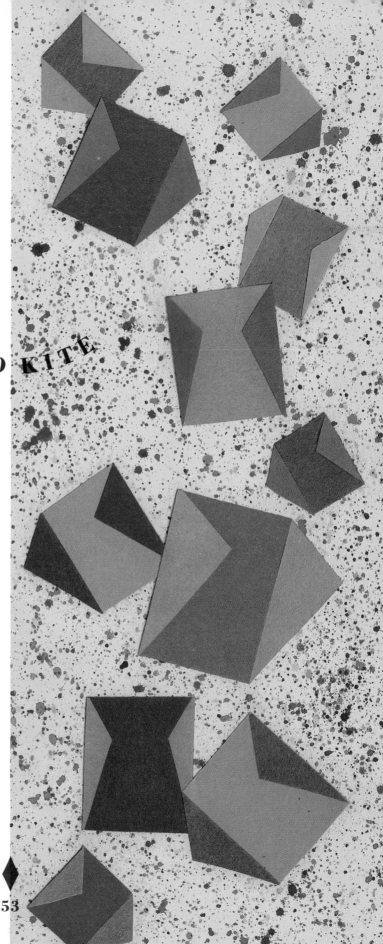

# SLED KITE

One of the easiest kites to build is the sled kite. There are only two struts in its construction, so there are fewer parts to break should you crash it one time too many. The sled kite depends on the pressure of the wind to keep it open, and has two **keels** to add stability. It flies best in light to moderate wind conditions.

This kite can be made to any size. If you remember to keep it four units wide and three units long you shouldn't go wrong.

## Materials

- ♦ butcher cord or thin garden twine
- ♦ strong tape
- ♦ 1 sheet of strong paper or light cloth, (a green garbage bag will do)
- ♦ 2 strong, straight sticks of bamboo or wooden dowelling 1 cm (¼") in diameter
- ♦ decorating materials

**1** Draw the sail pattern on the material, according to the diagram. Cut it out and lay it flat on your work surface. Cut a vent as shown to provide stability.

**2** Tape the wooden dowelling to the sail. Using a small nail or other sharp object, punch holes in the corners. Reinforce the corners with tape.

**3** To make the bridle the right length, measure a piece of string about three times the length of the kite. Tie the ends through the holes in the corners.

**4** It is important that the flying line is tied to the centre of the bridle point. To find the centre, fold the corners together, then tie a loop at the mid-point of the bridle. Tie the flying line to the loop. You might want to attach a tail to the bottom centre of the kite, though this isn't necessary.

**5** Decorate the kite however you wish.

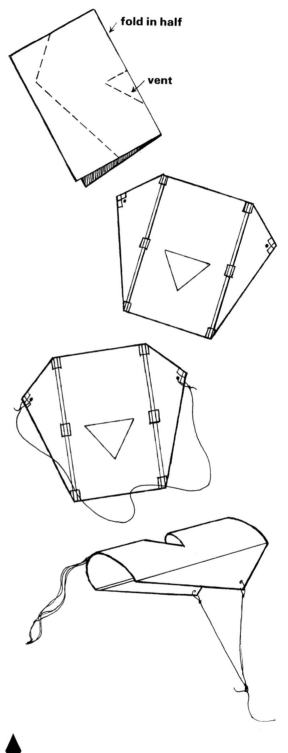

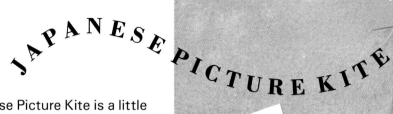

# JAPANESE PICTURE KITE

The Japanese Picture Kite is a little more difficult to make than the sled or diamond kite, but it is well worth the effort. With some patience, you can make a flying kite that can also be used as decoration.

## Materials

♦ light paper (**rice paper** or any other similar light but durable paper is good.)

♦ cotton string for the flying line

♦ bamboo strips or thin pieces of **balsa wood** .5 cm (1/8″) wide, cut to the following lengths:

> 2 × 45 cm (18″), with pointed tips as in the illustration
>
> 1 × 30 cm (12″), also with pointed tips as in the illustration
>
> 1 × 40.5 cm (16″)
>
> 2 × 25 cm (10″)

♦ glue

♦ poster paints or water colours

If you choose to use balsa wood, it is important to keep in mind that the struts need to be quite thin and flexible. You can shave the balsa wood strips down with a knife, but make sure that they are not so thin as to break under pressure.

**1** This kite can be made to any size, but for the sake of convenience, I've suggested some dimensions. On the paper draw a rectangle 30 cm × 42 cm (12″ × 17″), and cut the paper to this size.

**2** Paint any picture you wish on the paper using the poster paints or water colours. Leave a margin of about 2-3 cm (³/₄″-1″) around the edge of the paper.

**3** After your design is dry, turn it face down on the work surface. Fold over and glue down the left, right and bottom margins.

**4** Place the 30 cm (12″) long strut along the top margin, as in the illustration. Make sure the angle of the points is as shown.

**5** Glue the two 45 cm (18″) strips diagonally across the kite as shown in the illustration, with the points also angled as shown. Fold the top margin over the top cross-strut, making sure to overlap the diagonal struts at the top.

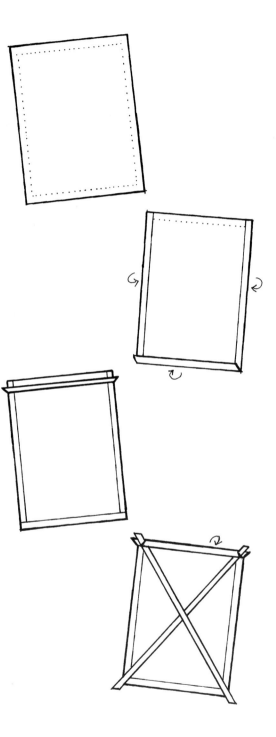

**6** Glue the 40.5 cm (16″) strut down the centre of the kite, making sure it crosses over at the intersection of the two diagonal pieces. Glue on the two 25 cm (10″) struts along the width of the kite, one 16.5 cm (6½″) from the top, the other the same distance from the bottom.

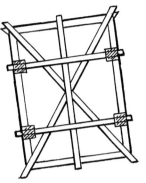

**7** Glue some small rectangular pieces of paper over the cross-struts where they meet the edge of the kite, as in the illustration. This will provide extra strength. Let the glue dry thoroughly before the next step.

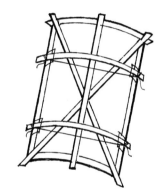

**8** Tie strings to the ends of the two main cross-struts, in such a way as to bow the kite slightly. They should resemble bowstrings.

Now that the main body of the kite is finished, it still needs to be bridled properly, that is, the flying line needs to be attached. This step needs patience.

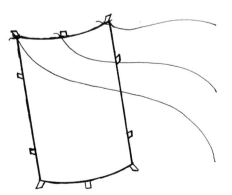

**a** Turn the kite back over so that the design is on top. Cut six 90 cm (36″) lengths of string. Tie three of them to the ends of the struts showing at the top as in the illustration.

**b** Using a small nail or any other such pointed object, punch three very small holes through the paper, one at the point where the struts cross over at the back of the kite, and one hole each at the point where the diagonal struts cross over the bottom cross-piece.

**c** Poke the remaining three strings through the paper, one through each hole, and tie them to the cross-pieces.

**d** Gather the ends of the strings together and adjust them so that the point at which they meet is approximately over the point where the strut that runs down the centre of the kite meets the top cross-strut. Tie the lines together tightly.

**e** Tie the flying line to the point where the bridle lines intersect.

This kite will fly better if you add two tails to the bottom corners of the kite. They should be two long strips of the same paper used for the sail, about twice the length of the kite itself.

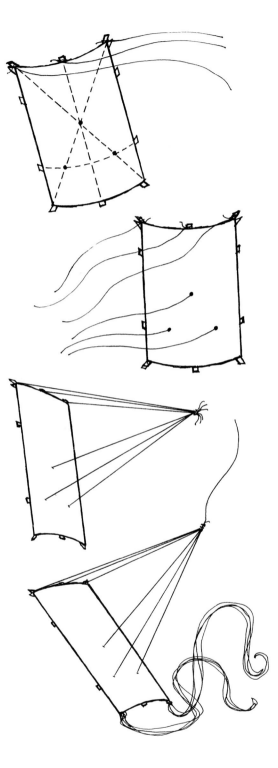

# Flying Your Kite

## Where and when to fly

Any open area which provides enough room (e.g. a field, playground, park or beach). Stay away from the base of large hills, or buildings and trees as they create turbulence.

Stay away from power lines, airports and road traffic!

Avoid very strong winds and stormy weather.

## How to launch your kite

With your back to the wind, hold your kite aloft and release it, remembering to allow the kite line to run through your hand as the wind takes the kite up. Keep a slight tension on the line while the kite is rising until it has reached the desired altitude, then grasp the line.

When the wind is too light for hand-launching, ask a friend to hold the kite 30 metres (100′) or more downwind from you, or prop the kite up, facing you, at the same distance. Wait for a breeze and then pull in on the line. The helper should release the kite as you pull in. The kite will rise and may catch enough wind. Let out a few feet of line, then pull some of it back in quickly to make the kite rise a little. Repeat this to make the kite rise. If the kite dives, quickly let out some slack. When it comes upright, pull in the line to make it rise again.

## Other tips

Tying a fishing swivel to the end of your line will make attachment to the bridle easier. The swivel will save you from tying knots and will help prevent twisting of the bridle and the line.

Wear gloves when flying hard-pulling kites to prevent burns from nylon line.

Carry items you need for repairs and adjustments — pocket knife, extra swivels, tail material, scotch tape, cloth tape, etc.

*(Used with the kind permission of Ray "The Wiz" Wismer, of Touch the Sky, Inc., Etobicoke, Ontario.)*

# Glossary

**B.C.E.** Before the Common Era.

**balsa wood** An extremely light and durable tropical wood.

**barkcloth** A felt-like type of cloth found in many tropical countries, made of tree bark that has been pounded soft.

**batik** cloth hand-printed by the Indonesian method of coating parts not to be dyed with wax.

**delta** A triangular kite.

**deva** A divine being in Hinduism and Buddhism. Devas, when appearing to mortals, never sweat nor blink, and neither do their feet touch the ground. They cast no shadows and wear ornaments made from never-fading flowers.

**foil** A type of kite which forms a pocket.

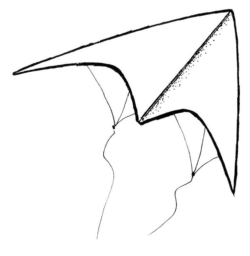

**glider** Similar to an aeroplane, without an engine.

**Hilo** A district on the island of Hawaii.

**keel** Fabric surface of a kite which adds stability when flying.

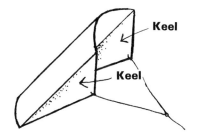

**Koi Nabori** A windsock in the shape of a carp, usually flown on Children's Day (May 5th) in Japan.

**Makar Sankranti** Makar Sankranti is the time when the sun moves into the Mankara constellation. Mankara is a mythological aquatic animal which looks a bit like a crocodile with the legs of a dog. It represents Capricorn in the Hindu zodiac.

**monsoon** A tremendous seasonal tropical storm accompanied by high winds and rain.

**Nagasaki Hata** A Japanese fighter kite, first developed in the city of Nagasaki.

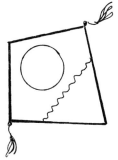

**olona** A tropical flower.

**rice paper** A paper made of pulverized rice, as opposed to wood pulp. It is very light and translucent.

**sail** Fabric covering of a kite which catches the wind.

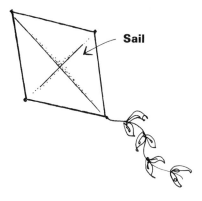

**Siva** (pronounced shĭ′va) A Hindu god who is male, female and neuter. Siva is the god of growth, destruction and regrowth.

**strut** A stick or strip of wood which forms the framework of a kite.

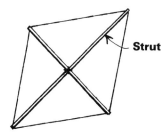

**tetrahedral cell** A tetrahedron is a four-sided pyramid-like shape. A tetrahedral cell kite is made up of many of these shapes.

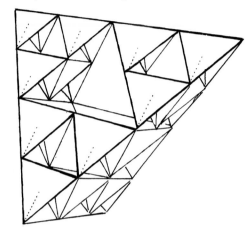

**train** A succession of kites all being flown on the same flying line(s).

**Vishnu** A major Hindu and Buddhist deity, Vishnu is believed to be the protector of the universe and the embodiment of goodness and mercy.

**Waimea** A district on the island of Hawaii.

**windsock** A long cylindrical cloth tube, open at both ends, attached at one end to a pole. It is usually used to indicate wind direction.

# Bibliography

Bahadur, Dinesh, *Come Fight A Kite*.
Fitzhenry & Whiteside Ltd., Toronto, 1978.

Burkhart, Timothy, *Kitefolio*.
Double Elephant, Berkley, 1974.
WildWood House, London, 1974.

Freidin, Simon, *Return to Bali*.
Kite Lines, Summer 1989.

Hart, Clive, *Kites: A Historical Survey*.
Paul P. Apple, Mt. Vernon, 1982.

Maysmor, Bob, *Te Manu Tukutuku: A Study of the Maori Kite*.
Allen & Unwin New Zealand Ltd., Wellington, 1990.

Miyawaki, Tatsuo, *"Tako" Japanese Kite Book*.
Biken-Sha, Hiroshima, 1962.

Morrison, Philip, *Kites of Makar Sankranti*.
Kite Lines, Summer 1989.

Pelham, David, *The Penguin Book of Kites*.
Penguin Books Ltd., Harmondsworth, 1976.

Peters, George, *Kites Over Ahmedabad*.
Kite Lines, Summer 1989.

Streeter, Tal, *The Art of the Japanese Kite*.
Weatherhill, New York, 1974.

Thompson, Vivian L., *Hawaiian Myths of Earth, Sea & Sky*.
Holiday House, New York, 1966.

◆

**David Evans** grew up in Barrie, Ontario. As a child he spent some time with his family in Nigeria, and has travelled extensively since.

He first developed his interest in kites when he worked at a kite store, and has taught kite making to pre-school and kindergarten age children.

David now works at the National Ballet School of Canada as a "den-father" in the students' residence. This job, as well as his two room mates, Anna Banana and Tom the Cat, make him very happy, as do the colours purple and green, beans on toast, and carrying baby Simon in a Snuggly.

**Adele D'Arcy** studied Fine Arts at Concordia University, and has lived and worked in her native Toronto ever since. She began exhibiting her paintings at an early age. Her illustrations have appeared in a variety of publications.

While Adele dislikes weather in general, she nevertheless enjoys long walks. Other favourite pastimes are photographing and drawing urban landscapes.

In addition to the above, Adele is fond of the colour black, and Oliver, the "eminence grise" in her life.